ULTIMATE BORON CURE

Separating Fact from Fiction for Optimal Health

Dye Mark

Copyright © 2024

All Rights Are Reserved

The content in this book may not be reproduced, duplicated, or transferred without the express written permission of the author or publisher. Under no circumstances will the publisher or author be held liable or legally responsible for any losses, expenditures, or damages incurred directly or indirectly as a consequence of the information included in this book.

Legal Remarks

Copyright protection applies to this publication. It is only intended for personal use. No piece of this work may be modified, distributed, sold, quoted, or paraphrased without the author's or publisher's consent.

Disclaimer Statement

Please keep in mind that the contents of this booklet are meant for educational and recreational purposes. Every effort has been made to offer accurate, up-to-date, reliable, and thorough information. There are, however, no stated or implied assurances of any kind. Readers understand that the author is providing competent counsel. The content in this book originates from several sources. Please seek the opinion of a competent professional before using any of the tactics outlined in this book. By reading this book, the reader agrees that the author will not be held accountable for any direct or indirect damages resulting from the use of the information contained therein, including, but not limited to, errors, omissions, or inaccuracies.

Table of Contents

INTRODUCTION 1

UNDERSTANDING BORON: AN ESSENTIAL ELEMENT 3

    What is Boron? 3

    The Importance of Boron in Health 4

    Historical Perspective on Boron's Uses 5

ATOMIC STRUCTURE AND PROPERTIES 6

    Atomic Structure of Boron 6

    Physical and Chemical Properties 7

OCCURRENCE AND EXTRACTION 10

    Natural Sources of Boron 10

    Methods of Extraction and Production 11

BORON COMPOUNDS 13

    Overview of Boron Compounds 13

    Common Boron Compounds and Their Uses 14

INDUSTRIAL APPLICATIONS 16

    Industrial Uses of Boron 16

    Boron in Manufacturing and Production 17

BORON IN TECHNOLOGY AND ENGINEERING 19

    Boron in Electronics and Semiconductors 19

    Boron-Based Materials and Nanotechnology 20

ENVIRONMENTAL IMPACT AND SUSTAINABILITY 22

Environmental Concerns Related to Boron 22

Sustainable Practices and Recycling 23

BORON DEFICIENCY: CAUSES AND SYMPTOMS 25

Signs of Boron Deficiency in the Body 25

Factors Contributing to Boron Deficiency 26

Health Risks Associated with Boron Deficiency 27

THE HEALING POWER OF BORON 30

Boron's Role in Bone Health 30

Boron and Joint Health 31

Boron's Impact on Hormonal Balance 32

Boron's Antioxidant Properties 33

BORON IN DISEASE PREVENTION AND TREATMENT 36

Boron's Potential in Preventing Osteoporosis 36

Boron's Role in Arthritis Management 37

Boron's Effectiveness in Supporting Hormonal Health 38

Boron's Antimicrobial Properties 39

INCORPORATING BORON INTO YOUR LIFESTYLE 41

Dietary Sources of Boron 41

Supplements: How to Safely Integrate Boron into Your Routine 42

Lifestyle Practices for Maximizing Boron Absorption 43

BORON MYTHS AND FACTS 46
   Dispelling Common Misconceptions about Boron 46
   Clarifying Safety Concerns and Dosage Guidelines 47
CONCLUSION 50

INTRODUCTION

Welcome to "Ultimate Boron Cure"! If you're holding this book, chances are you're on a quest for answers, searching for that elusive remedy to ease your woes and restore your vitality. Well, my friend, you've come to the right place. But before we dive into the nitty-gritty of boron's magical properties, let's have a little heart-to-heart.

Have you ever felt like your body is sending out distress signals in Morse code, and you're just not fluent in Morse? That's how it often feels when our health starts to take a nosedive. Maybe you've been grappling with mysterious joint pains, hormonal imbalances that make you feel like a rollercoaster on steroids, or perhaps you're just tired of feeling bone-weary all the time. Whatever it is, I get it. I've been there, too.

Picture this: It's 2 AM, and you're scrolling through endless web pages, desperately trying to decode your symptoms. You stumble upon a forum where someone swears by the miraculous powers of boron. Boron? Isn't that something from a high school chemistry class? But in your desperation, you're willing to give anything a shot. And hey, who knows? Maybe boron is the secret weapon you've been searching for all along.

Now, before you start sprinkling boron dust on your morning cereal (please don't), let's take a step back and explore what this element is all about. In "Ultimate Boron Cure," we're not just throwing random solutions at you and hoping they stick. No sire! We're delving deep into the science behind boron, unpacking its mysteries, and unlocking its potential to transform your health.

But let's get real for a moment. We're not promising overnight miracles or instant fixes. If you're looking for a magical potion that will whisk away all your health woes in the blink of an eye, you might be better off searching for leprechauns at the end of a rainbow. What we are offering is something far more valuable: knowledge, understanding, and a roadmap to navigate your way back to wellness.

In "Ultimate Boron Cure," we're not just your tour guides; we're your fellow travelers on this journey to better health. We've laughed in the face of confusion, shed tears of frustration, and shared moments of triumph with countless individuals who have walked this path before you. So believe me when I say, I understand how you feel. And I'm here to tell you that there's hope.

Throughout these pages, you'll find a treasure trove of information about boron—what it is, why it matters, and how it can be your ally in the battle for better health. We'll debunk myths, unravel mysteries, and equip you with the tools you need to harness the power of boron in your own life.

But hey, this isn't your typical stuffy science lecture. We're bringing the fun to the table, sprinkling in a healthy dose of humor and a pinch of irreverence along the way. After all, if we're going to talk about boron, we might as well have a good time doing it, right?

So grab a cozy blanket, brew yourself a cup of your favorite beverage (bonus points if it's boron-infused), and let's embark on this adventure together. Whether you're a seasoned health enthusiast or a newbie to the world of wellness, there's something here for everyone.

Remember, you're not alone on this journey. "Ultimate Boron Cure" is more than just a book it's a lifeline, a beacon of hope in a sea of uncertainty. So let's dive in and discover the transformative power of boron, one page at a time.

UNDERSTANDING BORON: AN ESSENTIAL ELEMENT

Boron might not be a household name like calcium or magnesium, but make no mistake—it's a true unsung hero when it comes to your health. In this chapter, we'll embark on a journey to unravel the mysteries of boron, exploring its significance, its historical roots, and its role as a vital nutrient for our well-being.

What is Boron?

Let's start with the basics. Boron is a chemical element found in nature, nestled snugly on the periodic table with the symbol "B" and atomic number 5. It's not as abundant as some other elements, but don't let its modest presence fool you, boron punches well above its weight in terms of importance.

In its natural state, boron exists in various forms, from crystalline compounds to amorphous powders. It's typically found in soil, water, plants, and even in some foods we consume. But what exactly does boron do in our bodies?

Well, buckle up, because boron wears many hats when it comes to supporting our health. It plays a crucial role in bone metabolism, helping to regulate calcium and magnesium levels and promoting bone growth and maintenance. Boron also has anti-inflammatory properties, making it a valuable ally in the fight against conditions like arthritis and osteoporosis. But that's not all, boron is also involved in processes like wound healing, hormone regulation, and brain function. In short, it's a multitasking marvel that deserves a spot in your nutritional toolkit.

Now, you might be wondering how much boron you need to keep your body humming along smoothly. The truth is, there's still some debate among experts about the optimal intake of boron. However, most agree that a daily dose of around 3 to 6 milligrams is sufficient for most adults. Of course, individual needs may vary depending on factors like age, sex, and overall health status, so it's always a good idea to consult with a healthcare professional to determine the right dosage for you.

The Importance of Boron in Health

So, why should you care about boron? Well, besides the fact that it's involved in a slew of essential bodily functions, there's mounting evidence to suggest that boron deficiency could spell trouble for your health.

Research has shown that inadequate intake of boron may be linked to an increased risk of certain health conditions, including osteoporosis, arthritis, and hormonal imbalances. Without enough boron in your system, your bones may become more prone to fractures, your joints may become inflamed and painful, and your hormones may go haywire, leaving you feeling out of sorts.

But fear not, dear reader, for boron is here to save the day! By ensuring that you're getting enough boron through your diet or supplementation, you can help safeguard your health and reduce your risk of falling prey to these pesky ailments.

Historical Perspective on Boron's Uses

Now, let's take a trip down memory lane and explore the fascinating history of boron's uses. Believe it or not, humans have been tapping into the power of boron for centuries, long before we even knew what it was. Ancient civilizations, including the Egyptians, Greeks, and Romans, were among the first to discover boron's remarkable properties. They used borax, a naturally occurring compound containing boron, for a variety of purposes, from preserving mummies to soldering metals. In China, borax was prized for its medicinal properties, believed to treat everything from skin conditions to eye infections.

Fast forward to the modern era, and boron's versatility has only continued to impress. Today, boron and its derivatives are used in a wide range of industries, including agriculture, medicine, and manufacturing. From fertilizers that boost crop yields to glass and ceramic production, boron plays a pivotal role in countless applications that touch our daily lives

But perhaps most exciting of all is the growing body of research uncovering the potential health benefits of boron. As scientists delve deeper into its mechanisms of action, we're gaining a better understanding of how boron can support our well-being and enhance our quality of life.

In conclusion, boron may not always steal the spotlight, but make no mistake, it's a nutritional powerhouse that deserves our attention. By understanding the role of boron in our bodies, recognizing its importance in maintaining optimal health, and appreciating its rich historical legacy, we can harness the full potential of this remarkable element to lead happier, healthier lives.

ATOMIC STRUCTURE AND PROPERTIES

Boron, with its atomic number 5 and symbol B, is a fascinating element with a unique atomic structure and a diverse range of physical and chemical properties. Understanding the atomic structure of boron is essential to grasp its behavior in various contexts, from industrial applications to biological processes. Additionally, exploring its physical and chemical properties sheds light on its role in the world around us and its potential applications in different fields.

Atomic Structure of Boron

The atomic structure of boron is relatively simple yet intriguing. With five protons in its nucleus, it belongs to the group of elements known as metalloids, which exhibit properties of both metals and nonmetals. Boron's atomic structure also includes five electrons, arranged in two electron shells. The first shell accommodates two electrons, while the second shell holds the remaining three electrons.

One of the notable characteristics of boron's atomic structure is its electron configuration. Boron has an electron configuration of $1s^2\ 2s^2\ 2p^1$, indicating that it has two electrons in the 1s orbital, two electrons in the 2s orbital, and one electron in the 2p orbital. This configuration gives boron unique chemical properties, particularly in its bonding behavior.

Boron's atomic structure contributes to its ability to form covalent bonds with other elements. Covalent bonds involve the sharing of electrons between atoms, and boron's three valence electrons make it highly reactive in forming these bonds. This reactivity is central to many of boron's chemical properties, allowing it to participate in a wide range of chemical reactions and form diverse compounds.

Moreover, boron exhibits several allotropic forms, meaning it can exist in different physical structures with varying properties. These include amorphous boron and crystalline forms such as rhombohedral boron and tetragonal boron. Each allotrope has its unique arrangement of boron atoms, influencing its physical and chemical behavior.

Understanding boron's atomic structure is crucial for elucidating its role in various applications, including its use in materials science, electronics, and medicine. By exploring the intricacies of its electron arrangement and bonding behavior, researchers can harness boron's unique properties to develop innovative technologies and materials for diverse purposes.

Physical and Chemical Properties

Boron exhibits a range of physical and chemical properties that contribute to its versatility and utility in various contexts. These properties stem from its atomic structure and bonding behavior, as well as its interactions with other elements and compounds.

One of the most notable physical properties of boron is its hardness. Crystalline forms of boron, such as rhombohedral boron, are extremely hard and have high melting points, making them valuable materials for applications requiring strength and durability. Boron's hardness also makes it useful in abrasives and cutting tools, where it can withstand high temperatures and pressures.

In addition to its hardness, boron is also lightweight, with a density lower than that of most metals. This combination of hardness and low density makes boron attractive for use in aerospace and automotive applications, where lightweight yet durable materials are essential for improving fuel efficiency and performance.

Boron's chemical properties are equally diverse and significant. As a metalloid, boron exhibits both metallic and nonmetallic characteristics, allowing it to form a wide range of compounds with other elements. One of the most well-known boron compounds is borax, a naturally occurring mineral commonly used in household cleaning products and as a flux in welding.

Boron compounds also play crucial roles in industries such as agriculture, where they are used as micronutrient fertilizers to enhance crop growth and yield. Boron's ability to form stable complexes with organic molecules makes it an essential element for plant nutrition, ensuring proper development and metabolism.

Moreover, boron's chemical properties extend to its role in materials science and nanotechnology. Boron-based materials exhibit unique electronic, optical, and mechanical properties, making them promising candidates for applications in electronics, sensors, and energy storage devices.

In summary, boron's physical and chemical properties make it a versatile and valuable element with diverse applications across various industries. From its hardness and lightweight nature to its ability to form complex compounds, boron continues to play a critical role in advancing technology, enhancing agriculture, and improving everyday products. Understanding and harnessing these properties are essential for unlocking the full potential of boron in the modern world.

OCCURRENCE AND EXTRACTION

Boron, though relatively rare in the Earth's crust, is found in various natural sources and can be extracted using different methods. Understanding the occurrence of boron and the techniques for its extraction and production is essential for ensuring a sustainable supply of this valuable element.

Natural Sources of Boron

Boron is primarily found in the Earth's crust in the form of borate minerals, which are compounds containing boron, oxygen, and other elements. These minerals are typically formed through the weathering and alteration of rocks containing boron-rich compounds. Some of the most common borate minerals include borax (sodium tetra borate), kernite (sodium borate hydrate), and ulexite (sodium calcium borate hydrate).

These minerals are often found in arid regions where the climate and geological conditions are conducive to their formation. Borate deposits can occur in sedimentary rocks, evaporate deposits, and volcanic regions, where boron-rich fluids have interacted with surrounding rocks over geological time scales.

In addition to borate minerals, boron is also present in seawater, albeit in much lower concentrations compared to terrestrial sources. The ocean serves as a reservoir for dissolved boron compounds, which are continuously cycled through geological processes such as erosion, sedimentation, and subduction.

Understanding the distribution and abundance of boron in natural sources is crucial for identifying potential mining sites and assessing the feasibility of extraction projects. Geological surveys and exploration efforts help pinpoint areas with high concentrations of borate minerals, guiding mining operations and resource management strategies.

Methods of Extraction and Production

The extraction of boron from natural sources typically involves mining borate minerals and processing them to isolate and refine the boron content. Several methods are employed in the extraction and production of boron, each tailored to the specific characteristics of the raw materials and the desired end products.

One common method of boron extraction is open-pit mining, which involves the excavation of large open pits to access borate deposits near the surface. This method is suitable for borate deposits located in arid regions with minimal vegetation and soil cover. Once the ore is extracted, it is transported to processing facilities for further treatment.

Another method used in boron extraction is underground mining, which is employed for deeper borate deposits that cannot be accessed through surface mining techniques. Underground mining involves the construction of tunnels and shafts to reach the ore body, followed by the extraction of the ore using specialized equipment. This method requires careful planning and engineering to ensure worker safety and minimize environmental impacts.

Once the ore is mined, it undergoes a series of processing steps to extract the boron content and refine it into usable products. These steps may include crushing, grinding, flotation, and chemical processing to separate the boron minerals from impurities and concentrate the boron content.

One of the primary methods used in boron production is the refining of borax ore through a process known as the boron-oxygen reaction. In this process, borax ore is heated with sulfuric acid to produce boric acid, which is then purified and crystallized to yield refined boron products. This method is widely used in commercial boron production due to its efficiency and scalability.

In addition to traditional mining and processing methods, there is growing interest in alternative approaches for extracting boron from unconventional sources such as geothermal brines and industrial waste streams. These methods offer the potential to recover boron resources from previously untapped sources and contribute to the sustainability of boron production.

Overall, the occurrence and extraction of boron involve a combination of geological exploration, mining operations, and processing techniques. By understanding the natural sources of boron and the methods used to extract and produce it, we can ensure a stable supply of this essential element for various industrial, agricultural, and technological applications.

ENVIRONMENTAL IMPACT AND SUSTAINABILITY

Boron, while being a valuable element with diverse industrial applications, also poses environmental concerns that need to be addressed. However, sustainable practices and recycling initiatives can mitigate these concerns, ensuring the responsible use and management of boron resources.

Environmental Concerns Related to Boron

One of the primary environmental concerns associated with boron is its potential toxicity to living organisms. While boron is an essential micronutrient for plants and some animals, excessive exposure to boron can be harmful, leading to adverse effects on human health and ecosystems. Boron toxicity can occur through various pathways, including ingestion, inhalation, and dermal contact, with the severity of effects depending on factors such as concentration, duration of exposure, and individual susceptibility.

In soil and water, elevated levels of boron can inhibit plant growth and reduce crop yield, posing challenges for agriculture and food security. Boron contamination in groundwater can also impact drinking water quality, posing risks to human health and necessitating remediation measures to ensure safe drinking water supplies. Furthermore, boron accumulation in aquatic ecosystems can disrupt aquatic life and ecological balance, affecting biodiversity and ecosystem services.

Industrial activities such as mining, manufacturing, and waste disposal can contribute to boron contamination of the environment. Mining

BORON COMPOUNDS

Boron compounds are a diverse group of chemical substances that play essential roles in various industrial, agricultural, and technological applications. From borax to boron-based polymers, these compounds exhibit a wide range of properties and functionalities, making them indispensable in numerous fields.

Overview of Boron Compounds

Boron compounds are chemical substances that contain boron atoms bonded to other elements or groups of elements. Boron is unique among the elements in its ability to form stable compounds with a wide range of elements, including hydrogen, oxygen, nitrogen, carbon, and metals. This versatility stems from boron's electronic structure and bonding behavior, which allow it to participate in a variety of chemical reactions and bond configurations.

One of the defining characteristics of boron compounds is their ability to form stable coordination complexes. Boron atoms can act as Lewis acids, accepting electron pairs from other molecules to form coordinate covalent bonds. This property enables boron compounds to serve as catalysts, ligands, and building blocks for a variety of chemical transformations and molecular assemblies.

Boron compounds are also known for their diverse structural motifs and geometries. Boron atoms can adopt various coordination numbers and geometries, ranging from planar trigonal to tetrahedral and octahedral arrangements. This structural flexibility contributes to the wide range of properties exhibited by boron compounds and their applications in fields such as materials science, catalysis, and medicine.

Common Boron Compounds and Their Uses

Boron compounds find applications in a multitude of industries and technologies, owing to their unique properties and functionalities. Some of the most common boron compounds and their uses include:

- **Borax (Sodium Tetra borate)**: Borax, also known as sodium tetra borate, is one of the most widely used boron compounds. It is primarily used in household cleaning products, laundry detergents, and as a flux in metallurgy and welding. Borax is also employed in the manufacture of fiberglass, ceramics, and fire retardants due to its high melting point and thermal stability.
- **Boric Acid**: Boric acid, a weak acid derived from borax, has numerous applications in industry and medicine. It is commonly used as an antiseptic and preservative in pharmaceuticals, cosmetics, and personal care products. Boric acid is also used in the production of glass, ceramics, and enamel coatings, where it serves as a flux and stabilizer.
- **Borates**: Borates, including borax and borax pentahydrate, are used as micronutrient fertilizers in agriculture. Boron is an essential micronutrient for plant growth and development, playing crucial roles in cell wall formation, carbohydrate metabolism, and reproductive processes. Boron-deficient soils can be treated with borate fertilizers to improve crop yield and quality.

- **Boron Nitride**: Boron nitride is a versatile compound with applications in electronics, ceramics, and lubricants. It exhibits properties similar to graphite, including high thermal conductivity and lubricity, making it suitable for use as a heat sink material and solid lubricant. Boron nitride is also used as a dielectric in electronic devices and as a refractory material in high-temperature applications.
- **Boranes**: Boranes are a class of compounds containing boron and hydrogen atoms bonded together. They are widely used in organic synthesis as reducing agents and catalysts for hydroboration reactions. Boranes also find applications in the semiconductor industry as precursors for boron doping in electronic devices.
- **Boron-Based Polymers**: Boron-based polymers, such as polyborazylene and polymeric boron nitride, exhibit unique thermal, mechanical, and electrical properties. These polymers are used in aerospace, automotive, and electronic applications, where lightweight yet durable materials are required. Boron-based polymers are also being investigated for use in energy storage devices and biomedical implants.

INDUSTRIAL APPLICATIONS

Boron plays a significant role in various industrial processes and applications, owing to its unique properties and versatility. From enhancing the strength of materials to facilitating chemical reactions, boron finds use in manufacturing, production, and numerous industrial sectors.

Industrial Uses of Boron

The industrial uses of boron are diverse and encompass a wide range of applications across multiple sectors. One of the primary industrial uses of boron is in the manufacture of glass and ceramics. Boron compounds, such as borax and boric acid, are added to glass formulations to improve thermal and chemical resistance, as well as to enhance optical clarity and strength. Borosilicate glass, which contains boron oxide as a major component, is used in laboratory glassware, cookware, and optical lenses due to its superior durability and thermal shock resistance.

In addition to glass manufacturing, boron compounds are employed in the production of fiberglass and insulation materials. Boron-based additives are incorporated into fiberglass composites to enhance mechanical strength, fire resistance, and thermal insulation properties. These materials find applications in construction, automotive, and aerospace industries, where lightweight yet durable materials are required for structural components and insulation.

Boron is also widely used in metallurgy and metallurgical processes. Boron-containing compounds, such as Ferro boron and boron carbide, are added to steel and other alloys to improve hardness, wear resistance, and machinability. Boron acts as a grain refiner and deoxidizer in steelmaking, helping to control grain size and reduce impurities, thereby enhancing the mechanical properties of the final product. Boron carbide is particularly valued for its extreme hardness and abrasion resistance, making it suitable for use in cutting tools, armor plating, and abrasive materials.

Furthermore, boron compounds find applications in the production of electronic devices and semiconductor materials. Boron is used as a dopant in silicon and other semiconductors to alter their electrical properties and create p-type semiconductor materials. By introducing boron atoms into semiconductor crystals, engineers can control the flow of electrical current and design electronic components such as diodes, transistors, and solar cells. Boron-doped silicon is essential for the fabrication of integrated circuits and electronic devices used in computers, smartphones, and other electronic gadgets.

Boron in Manufacturing and Production

Boron plays a crucial role in various manufacturing and production processes, contributing to the development of advanced materials, chemicals, and consumer products. One notable application of boron is in the production of boron-based polymers and advanced materials. Boron-containing polymers, such as polyborazylene and polymeric boron nitride, exhibit unique thermal, mechanical, and electrical properties, making them valuable for aerospace, automotive, and electronic applications. These polymers are lightweight yet durable, with high thermal and electrical conductivity, making them suitable for use in aircraft components, automotive parts, and electronic devices.

Boron is also used in the synthesis of specialty chemicals and pharmaceuticals. Boron-containing compounds serve as intermediates and catalysts in organic synthesis, enabling the production of complex molecules and pharmaceutical drugs. Boron-based reagents, such as boronic acids and boron esters, are widely used in cross-coupling reactions, Suzuki-Miyaura coupling, and other organic transformations, facilitating the synthesis of pharmaceuticals, agrochemicals, and fine chemicals.

Moreover, boron compounds find applications in the production of flame retardants and fire-resistant materials. Boron-based additives, such as borates and boron oxides, are incorporated into polymers, textiles, and building materials to enhance fire resistance and reduce flammability. These materials are used in construction, transportation, and consumer products to improve fire safety and meet regulatory standards for flame retardancy.

BORON IN TECHNOLOGY AND ENGINEERING

Boron's unique properties make it a valuable element in various technological and engineering applications, ranging from electronics and semiconductors to advanced materials and nanotechnology. Its versatility and reliability have positioned boron as a critical component in many cutting-edge technologies, driving innovation and progress in diverse fields.

Boron in Electronics and Semiconductors

In the realm of electronics and semiconductor technology, boron plays a crucial role in shaping the performance and functionality of devices. Boron is commonly used as a dopant in semiconductor materials, where it alters the electrical properties of the material and enables the fabrication of electronic components such as diodes, transistors, and integrated circuits.

When boron atoms are introduced into silicon crystals during the semiconductor manufacturing process, they create p-type semiconductor materials. P-type semiconductors have an excess of positive charge carriers (holes) and exhibit higher conductivity than intrinsic (undoped) silicon. This property allows engineers to control the flow of electrical current in electronic devices and design circuits with specific functions and characteristics.

Boron-doped silicon is widely used in the production of diodes and transistors, which are fundamental building blocks of electronic circuits. Diodes, for example, allow current to flow in only one direction and are used in rectifiers, voltage regulators, and signal processing circuits. Transistors, on the other hand, serve as amplifiers and switches, controlling the flow of current between different parts of a circuit.

Moreover, boron is essential for the fabrication of integrated circuits (ICs), which are the backbone of modern electronic devices. ICs consist of multiple interconnected electronic components, including transistors, resistors, and capacitors, fabricated on a single semiconductor substrate. Boron doping is used to create the p-type regions necessary for forming the transistor junctions and other components within the ICs.

In addition to its role in semiconductor manufacturing, boron is also used in other electronic applications such as solar cells and sensors. Boron-doped silicon is a key component of photovoltaic cells, where it helps convert sunlight into electrical energy by creating the necessary charge carriers for the photovoltaic effect. Boron-based sensors are employed in various industries for detecting and measuring parameters such as temperature, pressure, and gas concentration.

Boron-Based Materials and Nanotechnology

Boron's unique properties extend beyond its applications in electronics and semiconductors to the realm of materials science and nanotechnology. Boron-based materials exhibit a wide range of desirable properties, including high strength, hardness, thermal stability, and chemical inertness, making them ideal candidates for advanced engineering applications.

One example of boron-based materials is boron nitride (BN), a compound composed of boron and nitrogen atoms arranged in a hexagonal lattice structure. Boron nitride exhibits properties similar to graphite, including high thermal conductivity, electrical insulation, and lubricity. These properties make boron nitride suitable for applications in high-temperature environments, such as heat sinks, crucibles, and refractory materials.

Boron carbide (B_4C) is another important boron-based material known for its extreme hardness and abrasion resistance. Boron carbide is one of the hardest materials known, second only to diamond, and is used in a variety of applications requiring wear-resistant components, such as armor plating, cutting tools, and abrasive materials.

Furthermore, boron-based nanomaterials are of particular interest in nanotechnology due to their unique structural and electronic properties. Boron nanotubes, nanowires, and Nano sheets have been synthesized and studied for their potential applications in Nano electronics, sensors, and energy storage devices. These nanomaterials exhibit exceptional mechanical strength, thermal conductivity, and chemical stability, offering new possibilities for miniaturization and performance enhancement in various engineering applications.

operations, in particular, may release boron-containing compounds into the soil, water, and air, leading to environmental pollution and ecosystem degradation. Additionally, improper disposal of boron-containing wastes can result in long-term environmental impacts, requiring remediation efforts to mitigate contamination and restore affected ecosystems.

Sustainable Practices and Recycling

To address environmental concerns related to boron and promote sustainability, it is essential to adopt sustainable practices and implement recycling initiatives throughout the lifecycle of boron-containing materials and products.

One approach to minimizing the environmental impact of boron is through sustainable mining practices and resource management strategies. Responsible mining practices, such as minimizing waste generation, reducing water and energy consumption, and implementing pollution prevention measures, can help mitigate the environmental footprint of boron extraction and processing operations. Additionally, reclamation and rehabilitation of mined areas can restore ecosystems and support biodiversity conservation.

Recycling of boron-containing materials is another key aspect of promoting sustainability and reducing environmental pollution. Boron compounds such as borax, boric acid, and borosilicate glass can be recycled and reused in various industrial processes, thereby reducing the demand for virgin raw materials and conserving natural resources. Recycling initiatives for boron-containing products, such as electronic devices, fiberglass, and ceramics, can help recover valuable boron resources and minimize waste generation.

Furthermore, sustainable product design and manufacturing practices can contribute to reducing the environmental footprint of boron-containing products. Designing products for durability, recyclability, and resource efficiency can prolong product lifespan and minimize the generation of waste. Additionally, using alternative materials and technologies that have lower environmental impacts can help reduce reliance on boron and other potentially harmful substances.

BORON DEFICIENCY: CAUSES AND SYMPTOMS

Boron deficiency might not be a term you hear thrown around often, but make no mistake, it can have significant implications for your health and well-being. In this chapter, we'll delve into the ins and outs of boron deficiency, exploring the signs that your body might be lacking this essential element, the factors that can contribute to deficiency, and the potential health risks associated with inadequate boron intake.

Signs of Boron Deficiency in the Body

First things first, let's talk about how to spot a boron deficiency in the wilds of your own body. Unlike some nutrient deficiencies that come with obvious warning signs (hello, vitamin C and scurvy), boron deficiency can be a bit sneakier in its presentation. That's because boron doesn't have a flashy job like vitamin D (the sunshine vitamin) or iron (the oxygen carrier). Instead, it quietly goes about its business behind the scenes, supporting various physiological processes without much fanfare.

So, how do you know if your body is crying out for more boron? While there's no single definitive test for boron deficiency, there are some telltale signs that may indicate you're not getting enough of this vital nutrient. These can include:

- **Joint Pain and Inflammation**: Boron plays a key role in supporting joint health, so if you find yourself experiencing unexplained aches and pains in your joints, it could be a sign that your boron levels are running low.

- **Poor Bone Health**: Boron is involved in calcium metabolism and bone formation, so inadequate intake of boron may contribute to weakened bones and an increased risk of fractures.
- **Hormonal Imbalances**: Boron helps regulate hormone levels in the body, particularly estrogen and testosterone. If you're experiencing disruptions in your menstrual cycle, mood swings, or other hormonal issues, boron deficiency could be a contributing factor.
- **Cognitive Decline**: Some research suggests that boron may play a role in cognitive function and brain health. If you're noticing changes in your memory, concentration, or overall cognitive function, it's worth considering whether boron deficiency could be playing a role.
- **Skin Problems**: Boron deficiency has been linked to certain skin conditions, such as psoriasis and eczema. If you're struggling with persistent skin issues, it may be worth exploring whether boron supplementation could help.

Keep in mind that these symptoms are not specific to boron deficiency and could be caused by a variety of other factors. However, if you're experiencing any of these symptoms and suspect that boron deficiency could be a contributing factor, it's worth discussing with a healthcare professional.

Factors Contributing to Boron Deficiency

Now that we've covered the signs of boron deficiency, let's talk about what might be causing it in the first place. There are several factors that can contribute to inadequate boron intake or absorption, including:

- **Poor Diet**: Perhaps the most obvious culprit, a diet lacking in boron-rich foods can easily lead to deficiency. Boron is found in varying amounts in fruits, vegetables, nuts, and legumes, so if your diet skews heavily towards processed foods or lacks diversity, you may not be getting enough boron.
- **Soil Depletion**: Even if you're diligent about eating your fruits and veggies, you may still be at risk for boron deficiency if the soil in which they're grown is depleted of this essential nutrient. Industrial farming practices, soil erosion, and overuse of chemical fertilizers can all contribute to soil depletion, making it harder for plants to absorb boron.
- **Certain Medical Conditions**: Certain medical conditions or medications can interfere with the body's ability to absorb or retain boron. These can include gastrointestinal disorders, kidney disease, and certain medications like diuretics.
- **Age and Gender**: Some research suggests that older adults and postmenopausal women may be at higher risk for boron deficiency due to changes in hormone levels and decreased absorption of nutrients.

Health Risks Associated with Boron Deficiency

So, what's the big deal if you're deficient in boron? Well, as it turns out, quite a bit. Boron deficiency has been implicated in a number of health issues, ranging from musculoskeletal problems to hormonal imbalances and cognitive decline.

One of the most well-documented consequences of boron deficiency is its impact on bone health. Boron plays a crucial role in calcium metabolism and bone formation, so inadequate intake of boron can lead to weakened bones and an increased risk of fractures. This is particularly concerning for older adults, who are already at higher risk for osteoporosis and other bone-related conditions.

Boron deficiency has also been linked to joint pain and inflammation, which can be debilitating for those affected. Without sufficient boron to support joint health, individuals may experience stiffness, swelling, and discomfort in their joints, making it difficult to perform everyday tasks and activities.

Hormonal imbalances are another potential consequence of boron deficiency, particularly for women. Boron helps regulate estrogen and testosterone levels in the body, so inadequate intake of boron can disrupt hormonal balance and contribute to issues like irregular menstrual cycles, mood swings, and low libido.

Cognitive decline is yet another area where boron deficiency may exert its influence. Some research suggests that boron plays a role in cognitive function and brain health, so deficiency could potentially contribute to memory problems, difficulty concentrating, and other cognitive issues.

In addition to these health risks, boron deficiency has also been implicated in certain skin conditions, digestive problems, and immune system dysfunction. Clearly, ensuring an adequate intake of boron is essential for maintaining overall health and well-being.

boron deficiency is a real and potentially serious issue that can have far-reaching consequences for your health. By being aware of the signs of boron deficiency, understanding the factors that can contribute to it, and taking steps to ensure an adequate intake of boron through diet or supplementation, you can help safeguard your health and reduce your risk of experiencing the negative effects of deficiency. As always, if you have concerns about your boron status or any other aspect of your health, don't hesitate to reach out to a healthcare professional for guidance and support.

THE HEALING POWER OF BORON

Boron may not be the most glamorous nutrient on the block, but don't let its unassuming nature fool you, this little element packs a powerful punch when it comes to supporting your health and well-being. In this chapter, we'll explore the myriad ways in which boron works its magic, from promoting strong bones and healthy joints to balancing hormones and fighting oxidative stress.

Boron's Role in Bone Health

Let's start with one of boron's most well-known claims to fame: its role in promoting bone health. You see, boron isn't content to just sit on the sidelines, it's an active participant in the ongoing battle to keep your skeleton strong and sturdy.

So, how does boron work its bone-boosting magic? Well, for starters, boron helps regulate the metabolism of key bone-building nutrients like calcium and magnesium. By ensuring that these minerals are properly absorbed and utilized by your body, boron helps lay the foundation for strong, healthy bones.

But that's not all, boron also plays a role in stimulating the production of certain hormones that are involved in bone formation. Specifically, boron has been shown to increase the levels of estrogen and testosterone in the body, both of which are important for maintaining bone density and preventing osteoporosis.

In addition to its direct effects on bone metabolism, boron may also help reduce inflammation in the body, which can further support bone health. By calming the fires of inflammation, boron may help protect against conditions like arthritis and osteoarthritis, which can erode bone tissue over time.

So, if you're looking to keep your bones strong and healthy well into old age, don't overlook the importance of boron in your diet. Whether you're getting your daily dose from foods like fruits, vegetables, nuts, and legumes, or supplementing with a high-quality boron supplement, ensuring an adequate intake of this essential nutrient is key to maintaining optimal bone health.

Boron and Joint Health

But wait, there's more! Boron isn't just a one-trick pony when it comes to supporting your musculoskeletal system, it's also a key player in promoting healthy joints. If you've ever experienced the discomfort of achy, creaky joints, you'll be glad to know that boron may offer some much-needed relief.

So, how does boron work its joint-soothing magic? One way is by helping to maintain the structural integrity of joint tissues like cartilage and synovial fluid. By supporting the health of these tissues, boron can help reduce friction and inflammation in the joints, easing discomfort and improving mobility.

But that's not all, boron may also help reduce levels of inflammatory markers in the body, further alleviating joint pain and stiffness. By calming the fires of inflammation, boron can help protect against conditions like arthritis and rheumatism, which can wreak havoc on your joints and leave you feeling sidelined.

In addition to its direct effects on joint health, boron may also play a role in supporting overall musculoskeletal function. Some research suggests that boron may help improve muscle coordination and strength, which can further enhance mobility and reduce the risk of injury.

So, if you're tired of living with the constant ache of stiff, sore joints, it might be time to give boron a try. Whether you're getting your daily dose from foods like leafy greens, almonds, and avocados, or supplementing with a boron capsule, adding this powerful nutrient to your routine could be just what your joints need to feel their best.

Boron's Impact on Hormonal Balance

Now, let's talk hormones. You know, those elusive chemical messengers that seem to hold the keys to everything from mood swings to metabolism. Well, it turns out that boron may play a bigger role in hormonal balance than you might think.

First off, let's talk about estrogen. This hormone plays a crucial role in everything from reproductive health to bone density to mood regulation. And guess what? Boron may help support healthy estrogen levels in the body.

Some research suggests that boron may increase the production of estrogen, which could be beneficial for women going through menopause or experiencing hormonal imbalances. By boosting estrogen levels, boron may help alleviate symptoms like hot flashes, night sweats, and mood swings, allowing women to navigate this transitional phase with greater ease.

But that's not all, boron may also have a similar effect on testosterone, the primary male sex hormone. Research has shown that boron supplementation may increase testosterone levels in men, which could have a range of benefits, from improving muscle mass and strength to enhancing libido and sexual function.

In addition to its effects on estrogen and testosterone, boron may also play a role in regulating other hormones in the body, including insulin and thyroid hormones. By helping to maintain balance among these various hormonal systems, boron may promote overall health and well-being.

So, whether you're a woman navigating the ups and downs of menopause or a man looking to optimize your hormonal health, boron may be just what the doctor ordered. Whether you're getting your daily dose from foods like broccoli, apples, and chickpeas, or supplementing with a boron tablet, adding this powerful nutrient to your routine could help keep your hormones in harmony and your body in balance.

Boron's Antioxidant Properties

Last but not least, let's talk about boron's antioxidant powers. You see, boron isn't content to just support your bones, soothe your joints, and balance your hormones, it's also a potent defender against oxidative stress, that sneaky culprit behind aging, inflammation, and chronic disease.

So, what exactly is oxidative stress? Well, think of it as the byproduct of the body's natural metabolic processes. As your cells go about their daily business, they produce molecules called free radicals, which can wreak havoc on your cells and tissues if left unchecked. Enter antioxidants, like boron, which swoop in to neutralize these pesky free radicals and protect your body from their harmful effects.

But boron isn't just any old antioxidant, it's a superstar in the world of free radical scavengers. Research has shown that boron has potent antioxidant properties, capable of neutralizing a wide range of free radicals and protecting against oxidative damage.

But that's not all, boron may also help enhance the activity of other antioxidants in the body, further bolstering your body's defenses against oxidative stress. By working in tandem with other antioxidants like vitamin C, vitamin E, and glutathione, boron helps create a powerful antioxidant network that keeps your cells healthy and resilient.

In addition to its direct antioxidant effects, boron may also help reduce inflammation in the body, further protecting against oxidative damage. By calming the fires of inflammation, boron can help prevent the chronic low-grade inflammation that contributes to a wide range of health problems, from heart disease to cancer to neurodegenerative disorders.

So, if you're looking for a natural way to protect your body from the ravages of oxidative stress, look no further than boron. Whether you're getting your daily dose from foods like raisins, prunes, and almonds, or supplementing with a boron capsule, adding this powerful antioxidant to your routine could help keep you feeling young, vibrant, and full of life.

boron is a true powerhouse when it comes to supporting your health and well-being. From promoting strong bones and healthy joints to balancing hormones and fighting oxidative stress, boron plays a wide range of roles in the body, each one essential for maintaining optimal health. Whether you're getting your daily dose from foods like leafy greens, nuts, and fruits, or supplementing with a boron capsule, ensuring an adequate intake of this vital nutrient is key to unlocking its full potential. So, here's to boron, the unsung hero of the nutritional world and a true champion of human health.

BORON IN DISEASE PREVENTION AND TREATMENT

In the world of nutrition, boron often flies under the radar, overshadowed by more well-known players like calcium and vitamin D. But don't be fooled by its humble reputation, boron is a nutritional powerhouse with the potential to prevent and treat a variety of diseases. In this chapter, we'll explore how boron can be a valuable ally in the fight against osteoporosis, arthritis, hormonal imbalances, and microbial infections.

Boron's Potential in Preventing Osteoporosis

Osteoporosis, a condition characterized by weakened bones and increased risk of fractures, is a major health concern, particularly among older adults. But fear not, boron may offer a ray of hope in the battle against this debilitating disease.

You see, boron plays a crucial role in bone metabolism, helping to regulate the absorption and utilization of key bone-building nutrients like calcium and magnesium. By ensuring that these nutrients are properly incorporated into bone tissue, boron helps maintain bone density and strength, reducing the risk of fractures and osteoporosis.

But that's not all, boron also helps stimulate the production of certain hormones that are important for bone health, including estrogen and testosterone. These hormones play a key role in maintaining bone density and preventing bone loss, particularly in postmenopausal women and older adults.

In addition to its direct effects on bone metabolism, boron may also help reduce inflammation in the body, which can further support bone health.

By calming the fires of inflammation, boron helps protect against conditions like arthritis and osteoarthritis, which can erode bone tissue over time.

So, if you're looking to keep your bones strong and healthy well into old age, don't overlook the importance of boron in your diet. Whether you're getting your daily dose from foods like fruits, vegetables, nuts, and legumes, or supplementing with a high-quality boron supplement, ensuring an adequate intake of this essential nutrient is key to maintaining optimal bone health.

Boron's Role in Arthritis Management

Arthritis, a group of inflammatory joint diseases, affects millions of people worldwide, causing pain, stiffness, and reduced mobility. But boron may offer some relief for those struggling with this chronic condition.

You see, boron has anti-inflammatory properties that can help reduce swelling and pain in the joints, making it a valuable ally in the fight against arthritis. By calming the fires of inflammation, boron can help alleviate symptoms and improve quality of life for arthritis sufferers.

But that's not all, boron also plays a role in maintaining the structural integrity of joint tissues like cartilage and synovial fluid. By supporting the health of these tissues, boron can help reduce friction and wear-and-tear in the joints, further easing discomfort and improving mobility.

In addition to its direct effects on joint health, boron may also help reduce levels of inflammatory markers in the body, further alleviating arthritis symptoms. By targeting inflammation at its source, boron helps protect against the progressive joint damage that can occur with chronic arthritis.

So, if you're tired of living with the constant ache of stiff, sore joints, it might be time to give boron a try. Whether you're getting your daily dose from foods like leafy greens, almonds, and avocados, or supplementing with a boron capsule, adding this powerful nutrient to your routine could be just what your joints need to feel their best.

Boron's Effectiveness in Supporting Hormonal Health

Hormonal imbalances can wreak havoc on your health, leading to a wide range of symptoms and complications. But fear not, boron may offer some relief for those struggling with hormonal issues.

You see, boron plays a crucial role in regulating hormone levels in the body, particularly estrogen and testosterone. By helping to maintain balance among these various hormonal systems, boron can help alleviate symptoms like irregular menstrual cycles, mood swings, and low libido. But that's not all, boron may also help stimulate the production of certain hormones that are important for overall health and well-being. Some research suggests that boron supplementation may increase testosterone levels in men, which could have a range of benefits, from improving muscle mass and strength to enhancing libido and sexual function.

In addition to its effects on estrogen and testosterone, boron may also play a role in regulating other hormones in the body, including insulin and thyroid hormones. By supporting the health of these hormonal systems, boron helps promote overall hormonal balance and reduce the risk of associated health problems.

So, whether you're a woman struggling with the ups and downs of menopause or a man looking to optimize your hormonal health, boron may be just what the doctor ordered. Whether you're getting your daily dose from foods like broccoli, apples, and chickpeas, or supplementing with a boron tablet, adding this powerful nutrient to your routine could help keep your hormones in harmony and your body in balance.

Boron's Antimicrobial Properties

Last but not least, let's talk about boron's antimicrobial properties. You see, boron isn't content to just support your bones, soothe your joints, and balance your hormones, it's also a potent defender against microbial invaders.

Boron has been shown to have antimicrobial properties, meaning it can help kill or inhibit the growth of bacteria, viruses, fungi, and other microorganisms. This makes boron a valuable ally in the fight against infectious diseases and microbial infections.

But how does boron do it? Well, for starters, boron disrupts the structure and function of microbial cells, making it difficult for them to survive and reproduce. By targeting the microbial cell membrane and interfering with essential cellular processes, boron helps stop infections in their tracks.

But that's not all, boron also helps boost the immune system, making it more effective at fighting off invading pathogens. By enhancing the activity of immune cells like macrophages and natural killer cells, boron helps strengthen the body's natural defenses against infection.

In addition to its direct antimicrobial effects, boron may also help reduce inflammation in the body, which can further support immune function. By calming the fires of inflammation, boron helps prevent the chronic low-grade inflammation that can weaken the immune system and make you more susceptible to infection.

So, whether you're looking to ward off the common cold or protect against more serious infections, don't overlook the importance of boron in supporting your immune system. Whether you're getting your daily dose from foods like whole grains, beans, and nuts, or supplementing with a boron capsule, ensuring an adequate intake of this essential nutrient is key to keeping your immune system strong and resilient.

In conclusion, boron is a true multitasking marvel when it comes to disease prevention and treatment. From supporting bone health and managing arthritis to balancing hormones and fighting off microbial invaders, boron plays a wide range of roles in promoting overall health and well-being. Whether you're looking to prevent disease or manage existing health conditions, adding boron to your nutritional toolkit could be just what the doctor ordered. So, here's to boron, the unsung hero of the nutritional world and a true champion of human health.

INCORPORATING BORON INTO YOUR LIFESTYLE

As we've explored in previous chapters, boron is a vital nutrient with a wide range of health benefits. From supporting bone health and hormonal balance to fighting inflammation and oxidative stress, boron plays a crucial role in maintaining optimal health and well-being. But how can you ensure that you're getting enough boron in your diet and lifestyle? In this chapter, we'll explore some practical tips for incorporating boron into your daily routine, from dietary sources to supplements to lifestyle practices.

Dietary Sources of Boron

One of the easiest and most natural ways to incorporate boron into your lifestyle is through your diet. Fortunately, boron is found in a variety of foods, making it easy to get your daily dose without relying on supplements. Some of the best dietary sources of boron include:

- **Fruits**: Many fruits are excellent sources of boron, including apples, pears, grapes, and raisins. These delicious fruits not only provide a sweet and satisfying snack but also deliver a healthy dose of boron to support your overall health.
- **Vegetables**: Leafy greens like spinach, kale, and Swiss chard are rich in boron, as are cruciferous vegetables like broccoli, Brussels sprouts, and cauliflower. By incorporating plenty of these nutrient-packed veggies into your meals, you can boost your boron intake while supporting your overall health.

- **Nuts and Seeds**: Almonds, peanuts, walnuts, and sunflower seeds are all good sources of boron, making them perfect for snacking or adding crunch to your favorite dishes. Sprinkle them on top of salads, oatmeal, or yogurt for an extra boost of boron and other essential nutrients.
- **Legumes**: Beans, lentils, and chickpeas are all rich in boron, as well as fiber, protein, and other important nutrients. Whether you're enjoying a hearty bean stew, a spicy lentil curry, or a creamy hummus dip, legumes are a tasty and nutritious way to get your boron fix.
- **Whole Grains**: Whole grains like brown rice, quinoa, and barley are not only rich in fiber and vitamins but also contain significant amounts of boron. Swap out refined grains for whole grains in your meals to increase your boron intake while supporting your overall health.

By including a variety of these boron-rich foods in your diet on a regular basis, you can ensure that you're getting an adequate intake of this important nutrient to support your health and well-being.

Supplements: How to Safely Integrate Boron into Your Routine

While getting boron from dietary sources is ideal, some people may find it challenging to consume enough boron-rich foods on a daily basis. In these cases, supplements can be a convenient and effective way to boost your boron intake. However, it's important to use caution when incorporating boron supplements into your routine, as excessive intake can have negative effects on your health.

When choosing a boron supplement, look for one that contains a moderate dose of boron, typically around 3 to 6 milligrams per serving. Avoid supplements that contain excessively high doses of boron, as these can increase the risk of toxicity and adverse effects.

It's also a good idea to consult with a healthcare professional before starting any new supplement regimen, especially if you have underlying health conditions or are taking medications that may interact with boron. Your healthcare provider can help determine the appropriate dosage of boron for your individual needs and monitor your progress over time.

When taking boron supplements, be sure to follow the recommended dosage instructions provided by the manufacturer. Taking more than the recommended dose of boron can increase the risk of adverse effects, including gastrointestinal upset, skin irritation, and hormone imbalances.

It's also important to remember that supplements are not a substitute for a healthy diet. While supplements can help fill in the gaps in your nutrition, they should be used in conjunction with a balanced diet rich in nutrient-dense foods.

Lifestyle Practices for Maximizing Boron Absorption

In addition to dietary sources and supplements, there are several lifestyle practices you can incorporate into your daily routine to maximize your body's absorption of boron:

- **Eat a Balanced Diet**: In addition to boron-rich foods, be sure to include plenty of other nutrient-dense foods in your diet, such as fruits, vegetables, whole grains, lean proteins, and healthy fats. A balanced diet provides the vitamins, minerals, and other nutrients your body needs to function optimally, including boron.

- **Stay Hydrated**: Drinking an adequate amount of water is essential for optimal nutrient absorption, including boron. Aim to drink at least eight glasses of water per day to stay hydrated and support the efficient transport of nutrients throughout your body.
- **Limit Alcohol and Caffeine**: Excessive alcohol and caffeine consumption can interfere with nutrient absorption and metabolism, including boron. Limit your intake of alcoholic beverages and caffeinated drinks to moderate levels to ensure optimal nutrient absorption.
- **Manage Stress**: Chronic stress can disrupt hormone levels and impair nutrient absorption, including boron. Practice stress-reducing techniques such as meditation, yoga, deep breathing exercises, or spending time in nature to support your overall health and well-being.
- **Exercise Regularly**: Regular physical activity not only supports bone health and hormone balance but also enhances nutrient absorption and metabolism, including boron. Aim for at least 30 minutes of moderate-intensity exercise most days of the week to reap the benefits for your health and well-being.

By incorporating these lifestyle practices into your daily routine, you can maximize your body's absorption of boron and support your overall health and well-being. incorporating boron into your lifestyle doesn't have to be complicated or challenging. By focusing on boron-rich foods, using supplements judiciously, and adopting healthy lifestyle practices, you can ensure that you're getting an adequate intake of this important nutrient to support your health and well-being. Whether you're preventing disease, managing existing health conditions, or simply striving to optimize your health, boron can be a valuable ally in your journey toward better health. So, here's to embracing the power of boron and taking proactive steps to support your health and well-being for years to come.

BORON MYTHS AND FACTS

In the world of nutrition, misinformation and myths can abound, and boron is no exception. Despite its importance for overall health and well-being, boron is often the subject of confusion and misunderstanding. In this chapter, we'll tackle some common myths about boron and separate fact from fiction. We'll also clarify safety concerns and dosage guidelines to ensure that you can make informed decisions about incorporating boron into your daily routine.

Dispelling Common Misconceptions about Boron

- **Myth:** Boron is a toxic substance that should be avoided.
- **Fact:** While it's true that excessive intake of boron can be harmful, the same can be said for many essential nutrients, including vitamins and minerals. In reality, boron is a trace mineral that is found naturally in soil and many foods. When consumed in appropriate amounts, boron is safe and beneficial for overall health.
- **Myth:** Boron is only important for bone health.
- **Fact:** While boron does play a crucial role in supporting bone health, its benefits extend far beyond the skeletal system. Boron is involved in a variety of physiological processes, including hormone regulation, inflammation reduction, and antioxidant activity. Research suggests that boron may also support cardiovascular health, cognitive function, and immune function, making it a truly versatile nutrient.
- **Myth:** You can get all the boron you need from food alone.

- **Fact:** While it's certainly possible to get an adequate intake of boron from dietary sources, many people may not consume enough boron-rich foods on a regular basis to meet their needs. Factors such as soil depletion, food processing, and dietary preferences can all affect boron levels in the diet. In these cases, supplementation may be necessary to ensure optimal boron intake.
- **Myth:** Boron supplements are dangerous and should be avoided.
- **Fact:** When used responsibly and in appropriate doses, boron supplements can be a safe and effective way to boost boron intake. However, it's important to use caution when supplementing with boron, as excessive intake can have negative effects on health. Always follow dosage guidelines provided by the manufacturer and consult with a healthcare professional before starting any new supplement regimen.

Clarifying Safety Concerns and Dosage Guidelines

- **Safety Concerns:** While boron is generally considered safe when consumed in appropriate amounts, excessive intake can have negative effects on health. High doses of boron can cause gastrointestinal upset, skin irritation, and hormone imbalances. In severe cases, boron toxicity can lead to symptoms like nausea, vomiting, diarrhea, and even organ damage. To avoid these risks, it's important to stick to recommended dosage guidelines and avoid excessive intake of boron supplements.

- **Dosage Guidelines:** The recommended daily intake of boron varies depending on factors like age, sex, and overall health status. In general, adults are advised to consume between 1 to 3 milligrams of boron per day, although some individuals may require higher doses to meet their needs. It's always best to consult with a healthcare professional to determine the appropriate dosage of boron for your individual needs.

When choosing a boron supplement, look for one that contains a moderate dose of boron, typically around 3 to 6 milligrams per serving. Avoid supplements that contain excessively high doses of boron, as these can increase the risk of toxicity and adverse effects.

In addition to supplementation, you can also increase your boron intake by incorporating boron-rich foods into your diet. Fruits like apples, pears, and grapes, as well as vegetables like leafy greens, broccoli, and carrots, are all good sources of boron. Nuts and seeds, such as almonds, peanuts, and sunflower seeds, are also rich in boron, as are legumes like beans, lentils, and chickpeas. Whole grains like brown rice, oats, and barley are another excellent source of boron, making them a valuable addition to any balanced diet.

while boron may not be the most well-known nutrient, its importance for overall health and well-being cannot be overstated. By dispelling common myths and clarifying safety concerns and dosage guidelines, we can ensure that individuals have the information they need to make informed decisions about incorporating boron into their daily routine. Whether you're looking to support bone health, balance hormones, or reduce inflammation, boron may be just what you need to take your health to the next level.

CONCLUSION

Throughout this journey into the world of boron, we've uncovered its hidden potential and shed light on its importance for overall health and well-being. From its crucial role in supporting bone health and joint function to its impact on hormonal balance and immune function, boron has proven itself to be a true multitasking marvel in the realm of nutrition.

Dispelling common myths and clarifying safety concerns, we've shown that boron is not only safe but also beneficial when consumed in appropriate amounts. By emphasizing the importance of a balanced approach to boron intake, whether through dietary sources or supplements, we've provided readers with the knowledge they need to make informed decisions about their health.

As we reflect on everything we've learned, it's clear that boron is more than just a trace mineral, it's a key player in the quest for optimal health and vitality. But our journey doesn't end here. Armed with this newfound understanding of boron's potential, we have the power to take control of our health and unlock our body's full potential.

In the words of Hippocrates, the father of modern medicine, "Let food be thy medicine and medicine be thy food." This timeless wisdom reminds us that the choices we make about what we put into our bodies have a profound impact on our health and well-being. By nourishing ourselves with nutrient-rich foods and supplements like boron, we can lay the foundation for a lifetime of vitality and wellness.

So, let us embrace the power of boron and the wisdom of Hippocrates as we journey forward on the path to better health. With knowledge, determination, and a commitment to self-care, we have the ability to transform our lives and create a future filled with vitality, energy, and abundance. Here's to your health, and to the boundless possibilities that lie ahead.

www.ingramcontent.com/pod-product-compliance
Lightning Source LLC
Chambersburg PA
CBHW070418230526
45471CB00006B/2871